Dad bought a camcorder.

The children had a race. Dad
made a video.

"Smile everyone," said Dad.

Dad went to the sports day. He took the camcorder.

He made a video of Wilma.

It was Jo's wedding. Dad took the camcorder.

He made a video of the wedding.

It was Mum and Dad's anniversary.
Wilma wanted to make a video.

Dad showed Wilma the camcorder.
"It's easy," he said.

Wilma made the video.
"It's easy," she said.

"Smile please!" said Wilf.

The children watched the race.

They saw the sports day.

They looked at Jo's wedding.

They laughed at Wilma's video.

They went to the tree house.
Wilma wanted to make a video.

Dad let her use the camcorder.

Wilma made the video. She saw
two men.

They were burglars.

The burglars were running away.
Wilma made a video of them.

"Call the police," she shouted.

Dad got the phone. He phoned
the police.

Wilma got the burglars on video.

The police came. They looked at
the video.

"Well done!" they said.

The police caught the burglars.
"Thanks to Wilma," said Dad.